ORCA FOOTPRINTS TEACHER GUIDE

by Tasha Henry

ORCA BOOK PUBLISHERS

ORCA FOOTPRINTS

Small steps toward big changes.

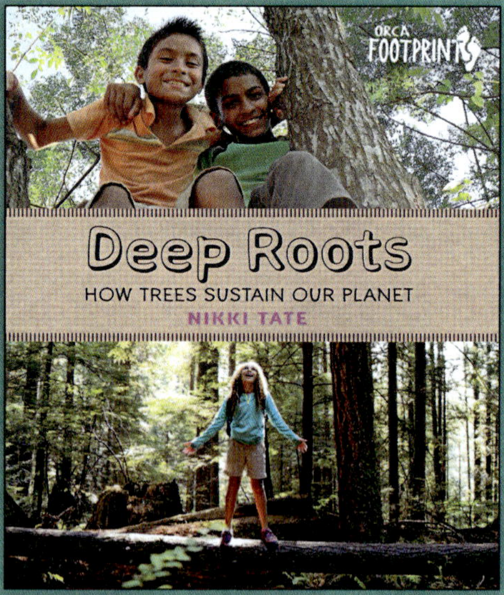

This teacher guide is a companion to the Orca Footprints series for ages 9-12. To order the series, please visit **orcabook.com**.

Orca Book Publishers gratefully acknowledges the support for its publishing programs provided by the following agencies: the Government of Canada, the Canada Council for the Arts and the Province of British Columbia through the BC Arts Council and the Book Publishing Tax Credit.

ORCA BOOK PUBLISHERS
orcabook.com

Printed and bound in the United States.

21 20 19 18 • 4 3 2 1

ORCA FOOTPRINTS TEACHER GUIDE

ORCA TEACHER RESOURCES

CONTENTS

Handouts and Assessment Tools 40

INTRODUCTION

As teachers, we are challenged to be creative and to model socially responsible practices with the resources we have. In Paraguay, for instance, a music teacher and a garbage picker created instruments made out of garbage from a local landfill for a children's orchestra. The group's first violin was constructed out of an oilcan, a fork and a few bottle caps. Now the Recycled Orchestra of Cateura travels the world, their music a unique example of collaboration, resourcefulness and sustainability.

In this age we have all come to understand that the things we consume, grow and throw away leave an environmental footprint. Everyday decisions, such as the food we buy or the items that we discard, affect all us, locally and globally. Think about that bag of grapes from Peru at the grocery store. How far did it travel to end up in your fridge? If you're in North America, it was 2,400 to 4,000 kilometers. Our daily decisions and actions reflect our responsibility to practice social, economic and environmental sustainability. But what does that look like in our classrooms and our school communities?

Around the world children are at the forefront of imagining and designing ethical solutions that support both local and global communities. Did you know that kids in Mexico play soccer with a ball called the SOCCKET? This innovative machine captures the energy of the soccer ball and after thirty minutes of playing can create enough power for three hours of light. There's a boy in Ohio who started recycling worn-out jeans to insulate houses for people in need. In Guatemala a bicycle called the Bicimáquinas uses the energy from pedaling to power water pumps and small appliances. In many ways, it already is the children who are leading us on the path toward sustainable living.

The Orca Footprints series invites you and your students to explore how our choices affect the planet and its people. With a few resources and a lot of imagination, young people are realizing how even small changes can make big differences. Practicing sustainability can be as simple as composting your leftover dinner scraps or buying non-toxic cleaning products for your home. There's no shortage of inspirational low-technology ideas from around the world. With this teaching guide, we invite you and your students to find new ways to reduce our individual and collective environmental footprints. We look forward to hearing about your work in your schools, homes and communities as compassionate and conscious global citizens.

Let's get to work!

USING THIS GUIDE

The Orca Footprints books are targeted to children aged nine to twelve. Through a blend of personal stories, thoughtfully researched information and captivating photographs, the authors weave stories about how our relationship to our basic needs creates a ripple effect around the world. The graphic design, image choices and personal stories are meant to appeal to a spectrum of abilities and interests.

The books work best in small, differentiated reading, research and inquiry groups so that all learners can imagine community-building opportunities while being inspired by initiatives already happening around the globe.

The Orca Footprints books overlap thematically and naturally dovetail. In this guide they are organized into "learning clusters" that focus on three simple sub-themes: Our Earth, Our Work, Our Global Community.

You can teach a book in isolation to complement a science, language arts or social studies unit, or use a learning cluster if you want an interdisciplinary approach to learning in your classroom. Each cluster offers teachers a variety of handouts, including thinking and assessment templates designed to encourage critical thinking, exploration and investigation through small-group engagement or individual inquiry. The entire series can provide a year-long theme for your school or classroom, as the books can engage all subjects and learning competencies.

Clusters of Learning

Learning Cluster One: Our Earth

This cluster focuses on how we grow, produce and consume food in relation to sustainable practices around the world. The work of generating food, from advanced farm technologies and livestock farming to growing vegetables on urban rooftop gardens, is explored through the way children are involved in food production. We expand from the concept of food to look at how green space in general and our friends the trees and bees help us build stronger communities. The suggested titles in this cluster are:

Let's Eat!: Sustainable Food for a Hungry Planet
Down to Earth: How Kids Help Feed the World
Going Wild: Helping Nature Thrive in Cities
Deep Roots: How Trees Sustain Our Planet
What's the Buzz?: Keeping Bees in Flight

Learning Cluster Two: Our Work

This unit dives into the ways children around the world are solving complex environmental problems through creative and collaborative science, design and technology innovations. The work done by children and adults who believe in sustainable energy sources is touched on in each book as a way to work toward sustainable living for all. The suggested titles in this cluster are:

Brilliant!: Shining a Light on Sustainable Energy
Every Last Drop: Bringing Clean Water Home
Pedal It!: How Bicycles are Changing the World
Take Shelter: At Home Around the World
Dive In!: Exploring Our Connection with the Ocean

Learning Cluster Three: Our Global Community

This cluster examines social justice, consumerism and social equity. Each title offers students the opportunity to reflect on the ways their beliefs and actions affect others around them. These books offer concrete and practical ways of supporting diversity in our local and global communities.

Pocket Change: Pitching In for a Better World
A Fair Deal: Shopping for Social Justice
Trash Talk: Moving Toward a Zero-Waste World
Better Together: Creating Community in an Uncertain World

Teaching to Diversity in the Classroom

We can't really talk about global citizenship and ethical interactions and actions unless we first make sure that all learners, with their unique strengths, feel they are contributing in the microcosm of the classroom and can access new concepts at the level they are able to. Shelley Moore's lesson templates and terminology were chosen as the foundation of the learning activities in this guide, to encourage a learning environment that prizes diversity and learning competencies over acquired knowledge or rote learning. As a way to strengthen inclusion in your practice, consider using the lesson planning and assessment templates provided by Shelley Moore on her website:
blogsomemoore.com/shout-outs/templates/

Instructional Terms

The guide offers a lesson sequence using these instructional terms:

- *Big Idea*: The over-arching concept(s).
- *Unit Guiding Questions*: The key questions for inquiry-based learning.
- *Lesson Goal(s)*: What most of your learners will be able to do, know or say after the study unit.
- *Connecting Activities*: Activities that invite your learners to make connections between their own life experience and knowledge base and the big idea.
- *Processing Activities:* Learning activities designed to stretch your students' thinking by encouraging them to demonstrate different ways of exploring their understanding of the concepts.
- *Transforming Activities:* Activities that challenge students to apply their knowledge in new contexts.
- *Extensions*: Activities that could lead to whole-class or individual long-term research projects.

Indicates an exercise with a handout available in the back of the book.

Learning Assessment

I use Shelley Moore's assessment language with my students to engage all learners at the level at which they can demonstrate their understanding and application of new concepts. You will see that my assessment tools use "I" statements and reflective questioning as a way to make learning personal and meaningful for each student.

At the beginning of each book, new concept or learning cluster, assess what your kids already know about an idea, concept or term by using any of the generic **concept maps** to generate thinking:

- Frayer Model
- Concept Tree
- Concept Quadrangle

To assess how your students formulate questions or research topics, use the **thinking templates:**

- World Map
- Project Proposal Outline
- Research Grid
- Key Question/Sub-Questions

At the end of each cluster or culminating activity, use the **assessment tools** (see page 40) to evaluate how each child has absorbed, connected, processed and transformed new information:

- KWL Chart
- Unit Assessment Demo
- Inquiry-Based Learning Rubric
- Self-Assessment Rubric

In conjunction with these tools, I love using **portfolio assessment** and reflective learning assessment to individualize the learning process.

Portfolio Assessment Checklist

✓ Create a table of contents or a checklist of required activities and assignments. Some items can be one-off handouts, and others can be larger inquiry projects or products. (See Inquiry-Based Learning Rubric.)

✓ Use interviews and one-on-one discussions to assess strengths and areas of growth.

✓ Use the Self-Assessment Rubric for authentic assessment of any product, culminating activity or inquiry project for the unit.

✓ Use ongoing reflections (writing in role or diary-like daily reflections) to document the learning journey.

✓ Think about learning as a continuum, not a destination. Trust that each child is exactly where they need to be.

Finally, the learning activities, not unlike the Footprints books themselves, are meant to engage all viewers/readers in an integrative and transformative learning experience. Dive deep, open up, and, most of all, have fun!

LEARNING CLUSTER ONE: OUR EARTH

This unit focuses on alternative and sustainable farming and urban growing practices by looking at the "stories" our foods carry on their way to our mouths. In examining the impact our food consumption has on the lives and well-being of others, we can begin to innovate simple ways of producing enough food for all the people around the world.

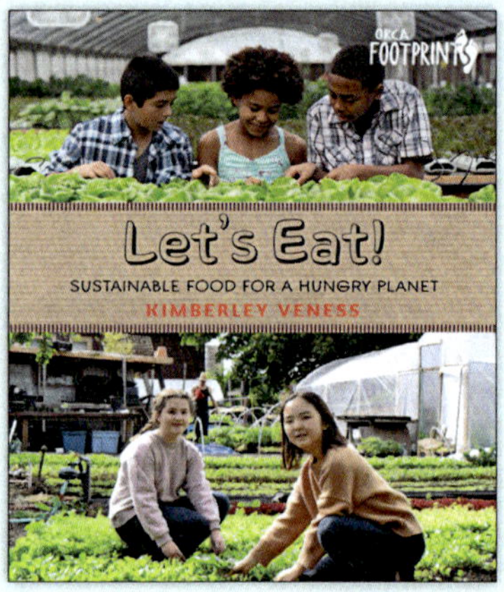

Book Title: *Let's Eat!: Sustainable Food for a Hungry Planet* by Kimberley Veness

Big Idea: The journey our food takes to get to our table can sometimes be very involved and have a huge environmental impact. If we are going to consider feeding all the people on the planet, we need to create alternative farming and growing technologies for sustainable consumption.

Unit Guiding Questions: Why is it important to know where our food comes from? What alternative farming practices around the world are changing the way we look at food production? What are some farming practices in your town or city that would be considered sustainable practices?

Lesson Goals: I know that Earth is an ecosystem connected by wind and water. I know that what I consume directly impacts others around the world.

Discussion Questions:

1. After reading chapter 1, discuss how the Industrial Revolution altered farming practices.
2. What is permaculture?
3. What is the environmental cost of consuming CAFO meat?
4. What is the more environmentally sustainable form of aquaculture?
5. What is the traffic-light color system that SeaChoice created for consumers of sustainable seafood?

Connecting Activity: Food-Travel Log

If you live in North America a lot of your groceries are traveling 2,400-4,000 kilometers (1,500-2,000 miles) to get to your grocery store.

Student instructions

1. Using the chart in the handout **"Food-Travel Log,"** take ten things out of your fridge, pantry or kitchen cupboard. Pick a mixture of fresh things (fruit, vegetables, meat, etc.) and packaged dry goods.
2. Record the country of origin. Using Google, calculate the distance in kilometers or miles from this country to you.

3. What patterns do you notice? What is the total number of kilometers or miles that all these products had to travel to get to you?

Processing Activity: Define the Terms

Student instructions

Using the book and working in small groups, fill in the glossary (see the handout "***Let's Eat!*: Personalized Glossary**").

Processing Activity: Fish, Meat, Vegetable

Teacher directions

1. Divide the class into three groups: fish, meat, vegetable. Have each student choose one type of fish, meat or vegetable to research. *Guiding questions*: Where did it come from? Under what conditions was it grown/raised? What journey did it take to get here?
2. Ask students to create a story map of the fish, animal or vegetable, using pictures or cut-out images from magazines to show the journey of that food item.
3. Have students write a first-person poem or narrative from the vantage point of the vegetable or animal that traveled that distance to become their food. Tell them to pretend they are a food—some sweet grapes in Mexico or some delicious kiwis in New Zealand, for example—and describe in first person their journey and how they ended up in someone's lunchbox.

Processing Activity: Family Menu

Student instructions

Use the "***Let's Eat!*: Family Menu**" handout to create a dinner menu for your household for one week. This menu should have as little impact as possible on the Earth. Pretend that money isn't an issue! Consider using local or sustainable produce, fish and meat, or simply minimize the consumption of meat or transgenic foods as a way to support the environment.

Transforming Activities: Chew on This!

1. Research farms in your area. Are you living in the city? Where is the nearest farm? Create a field trip to the nearest farm. Ask how students can volunteer.
2. Research a local farmers' market in your neighborhood. What organization runs it? Who are the vendors? Can your class visit?
3. Research how to build a school garden. How can your school support this initiative?

Transforming Activity: Consumer Family Challenge

Student instructions

Challenge your whole family to eat only what they have at home for five days. That means no Starbucks coffee for anyone! No soda from the vending machine! Everyone in your house must bring a lunch, a drink and all snacks with them to school and work. On Friday night discuss what it was like for all of you not to buy anything all week.

- What did you learn about yourselves?
- How much money did you save?
- What would you do together as a family with the money you would save if you extended this challenge to last for a few months?

Extension: Need or Want?

Student instructions

Create a fishbone chart of your family's needs and wants. Interview each member of your household and ask them to make a list of the things they want to buy that week. These items could be food, clothing or even registration fees for activities. Ask them to identify which items are needs and which items are wants. Examine your family's lists and present to the class which things you have determined, based on your data, are in fact needs. What did you learn? Does this activity shift your household's thinking about the difference between desires and necessities?

PAMELAJOEMCFARLANE/ISTOCK.COM

Book Title: *Down to Earth: How Kids Help Feed the World* by Nikki Tate

Big Idea: Children all over the world help grow and harvest food in ethical and sustainable ways. Farming, foraging and harvesting practices around the world teach us about sustainable ways of growing food and raising livestock.

Unit Guiding Questions: Why is genetic diversity important? What is the difference between a pet and a farm animal?

Lesson Goals: I know that children around the world participate in family and small-business farms. I can give five examples of sustainable farming practices. I know that genetic diversity supports sustainability.

Connecting Activity: Food Diary

Student instructions

1. Open your lunchbox. How many items are from a farm? How many items are from a *local* farm?
2. Using the **"Food Diary"** handout, keep a food diary for two days. Write down each ingredient in the category box.
3. Discuss as a class how much meat you consumed in total. How much dairy? What types of vegetables did you eat? What drinks did you consume?
4. Create a class chart tracking all consumption for thirty-six hours of items in the categories listed. What do our eating habits tell us about our demographics? Our choices? Our needs and wants?

Processing Activity: Read the Label

1. Read chapter 2 (as a read-aloud or individually).
2. Ask students to bring in the label on the egg carton in their family's refrigerator or take a picture of it and bring that. Where did their eggs come from? Ask them to research the farm. What are the differences between the different types of eggs in your local supermarket?
3. Conduct a boiled-egg taste test. Ask students which type of egg tastes and looks best to them.

Processing Activity: Word Sort

Using the **"How Kids Help Feed the World: Word Sort"** handout, divide the class into pairs and have them categorize as many forms of crops and livestock as they can!

Transforming Activity: Jam!

Everyone loves homemade jam, right? With a hotplate, some sugar and pectin, you can make a jar of jam in less than an hour. What fruits are seasonal in your area? Can you use frozen fruit? Are there any parents who are experienced canners who can help you?

Extension: Fermenting Fun

Every culture has a way of preserving food. Often salt or vinegar is used. Consider fermenting vegetables as a way to discuss natural ways of preserving local vegetables. Can you make sauerkraut or kimchi in your class?

Children pick fresh tomatoes at a farm in India.
NIKHIL GANGAVANE/DREAMSTIME.COM

Book Title: *Going Wild: Helping Nature Thrive in Cities* by Michelle Mulder

Big Idea: Communities around the world are "rewilding" their lifestyles and living spaces to build safer and more enjoyable places in which animals and humans can co-exist.

Unit Guiding Questions: How do humans benefit from nature? What does biodiversity look like from where you live? How are cities around the world designing green spaces for a sustainable future? What unique role do children play in planning and development to revitalize ecosystems in their neighborhoods?

Lesson Goal: I can identify five ways that I can bring nature and wildlife into my neighborhood.

Connecting Activity: Sidewalk Safari

Go for a classroom walk or a "Sidewalk Safari" (chapter 4, page 36). Ask each child to draw or take pictures of plants and animals they see on the walk. Catalog the items after researching their origins.

Connecting Activity: Reading and Viewing Together

Read the book aloud or do a shared reading in small groups. Experiment with the features in the book by using different speakers. Good readers can read the text, less confident readers can read the fact boxes, and non-confident readers can interpret the photos.

Processing Activities: Thinking Historically

1. Read chapter 1 as a class. Trace the development of the modern city by creating a timeline using the facts in the book. Use pictures and drawings to show the development of city structures from ancient Egypt until now. Do you live in a city or town? What makes your city sustainable?

2. Research the Indigenous peoples of your area. What practices can you identify that demonstrate a cultural alignment with nature? Invite an Indigenous elder into your classroom. How are Indigenous ways of knowing tied to the land and water? What plants are native to your area? What plants are invasive or imported?

Processing Activity: Wild Author

Have students read the biography of the *Going Wild* author, Michelle Mulder. Have each child write a letter to Michelle, sharing their proposal for how they want to make their school more "wild."

Processing Activity: Getting Greener

Read the book in small groups. Have each group present:

1. One way that children in another part of the world are making their community greener. Students will research the area, the people and the initiative.
2. One way students can make your classroom more green. It can be as simple as planting bean seeds in egg cartons on the windowsill or as complex as organizing a composting system at your school.

Transforming Activities: Going Wild for One Week

1. Read chapter 4. Using the "*Going Wild:* Five-Day Challenge" handout, create a grid showing what initiatives are already taking place at home, at school and in your city or town.
2. Wild challenge: Choose one aspect from your grid that you would like to take on for one week. Is it at home? Or at school? Perhaps it is personal. Detail your commitment with things that are achievable in one week. Post your challenge on a classroom blog!
3. Make a video about your five-day challenge. Document your journey, what you learned and the questions you are left with. Leave your audience with a "wild" challenge. Can you create your own community challenge? Post your video on your school or school board website.

Extension: Designing Green

Design challenge: Using landscape-design principles or software, design some green space for your school or home. This could be as simple as bee-attracting flower beds or potted cherry tomato plants on your rooftop. Submit your plans to the administration team or Parent Advisory Committee for consideration.

Book Title: *Deep Roots: How Trees Sustain our Planet* by Nikki Tate

Big Idea: Trees play an integral role in our ecosystem and our livelihood. Beyond their economic value, trees are important in creating healthy communities, both environmentally and socially.

Unit Guiding Questions: In what ways do trees sustain us? In what ways are we dependent on trees for our own survival? In what ways does our behaviour also affect the health of these ecosystems?

Connecting Activities: Leafy Collections

Teacher instructions

1. Have students collect leaves from the trees outside your classroom. Research the origin of their species. How do trees provide us with food, fuel, shelter, oxygen and water?
2. Ask each child to find one leaf from outside the school or in the area. (It could be a pine needle!) Then have them write on an index card the unique properties of the tree it's from and how it is connected ecologically to the survival of its forested friends. If it is a transported tree (not indigenous), tell its story! Ask each child to tape the sample to its index card. Put all the samples in a paper bag and have different people "pick a leaf" to read to the class. Can this lead to an in-depth botany lesson? A natural resources lesson?
3. Using the handout "***Deep Roots:* What We Do for Trees**," ask students to describe five things that we do for trees and five things that trees do for us.

Student instructions

1. Research different methods of slash-and-burn agriculture around the world. Name the countries where this happens. List the pros and cons of each method.
2. Write a letter to your president or prime minister from the vantage point of an indigenous tree species. What do you ask for? What practices are needed to ensure sustainable logging practices?

Book Title: *What's the Buzz: Keeping Bees in Flight* by Merrie-Ellen Wilcox.

Big Idea: Bees play an often unrecognized but essential part in the process of food production that humans depend on.

Unit Guiding Questions: How are bees important to biodiversity? How do bees impact habitats for animals and plants? In what ways are bees essential to our ability to source food?

Lesson Goals: I can explain in my own words how humans, plants and animals rely on bees. I know how bees work, how hives are made, different types of bees and the role of the queen bee.

Connecting Activity: Why Bees Are Important

Teacher instructions

1. Preview these videos: *What's happening to the bees: Why they are important* (youtube.com/watch?v=GWlq8vAeanQ) and *Kids learn why bees are awesome* (video.nationalgeographic.com/video/news/150815-kids-bees-pollinators-farms-vin)
2. After watching the videos as a class, ask students to recall eight reasons why bees are important.

Processing Activities: Bees at Work

Teacher instructions

Read chapter 2, "Bees at Work," out loud as a class. Ask students to work with a partner or individually to complete the **"Bees at Work: Fill in the Blanks"** handout. Instruct them to give their best explanations! If it is easier for them to draw diagrams to explain their thinking, encourage them to do that. Afterward discuss their answers as a class.

Answer Key: (1) stamen/pollen (2) pistil/pollination (3) conifers (4) yes/any logical answer (5) fruits, veggies, nuts and seeds (6) 15 (7) blue orchard mason bee (8) Plants that prevent streams and riverbanks from eroding depend on bees to pollinate them. (9) A grizzly bear's diet consists of two-thirds fruit in the summer, and it would have been pollinated by bees.

Student instructions

1. Read pages 39-43. Create an **oral presentation** that persuades kids in your class to support the bee population. Use the seven "tips" to outline seven simple things that kids in your community can do to support bees! Make a video to share with your school community.
2. Write a three-page, five-paragraph persuasive **essay or report** about the importance of our bee population. Use diagrams or drawings to show the important service bees provide for our food production. Present your report to another class or a younger grade. Can you bring in samples of honey for them to taste?
3. Create a list of questions and **interview a beekeeper** in your city or neighborhood. Report back to your class on what you learned from the interview. Post your interview questions and the responses in your classroom.
4. Celebrate your hard work with a local **honey-tasting contest**! Can you taste the flowers in each honey? Which honey tastes the best to you? Clover? Buckwheat? Manuka?
5. **Research** the origins of the plants that provide the bees with pollen. Can you recognize clover growing between the sidewalk cracks? Can you grow this plant for the bees in a small pot, a garden or a local greenspace?

Extension: Integrate it! Extending into Language Arts

1. Order a class set of the novel *The Summer We Saved the Bees* by Robin Stevenson. As a guided-reading novel study, or using literature circles, discuss the relevance of this novel in terms of the environmental impact of a dwindling bee population.
2. Read the book out loud to your class every morning over the duration of the Footprints unit. What does the story tell us about the power of children to change the world? Use ecological theory to support your arguments.

LEARNING CLUSTER TWO: OUR WORK

This unit dives deeper into practical and inventive ways of reducing our footprint and increasing our global perspective by building communities that share more and consume less. By focusing on conservation and innovation as platforms for sustainability, this unit looks closely at three action points: water, energy and recycling.

Book Title: *Brilliant!: Shining a Light on Sustainable Energy* by Michelle Mulder

Big Idea: Energy can be transformed!

Unit Guiding Questions: How is energy converted? How can energy be created and destroyed? What is clean energy? How can energy be sustained in my community for generations?

Lesson Goals: I can define what energy is and how it can be transformed using multiple ways of presenting my knowledge. I can define seven types of energy and articulate which energy sources are sustainable and renewable.

Connecting Activity: What Do We Already Know?

1. Define energy together on a large piece of chart paper, using symbols and words. Use different-colored markers. Include the definition "Energy is the ability to make things." Draw pictures to describe this definition.
2. Discuss as a group: Can energy be made and destroyed? What are some examples?

Connecting Activity: Exploring Sustainable Energy

Divide the class into four groups, one for each chapter of the book. Ask each group to create and present a poster on their chapter. Assess students on their abilities to speak and listen to each other.

Processing Activities: Collect your Energy

Teacher instructions

1. Working individually or in small groups, students will look through magazines and newspapers and cut out images or pictures they associate with the basic energy sources: fossil fuels, sun, wind, steam, organic compounds, water, electricity, fire, etc. They will then create a collage using these images. Post the collages around the classroom.
2. Discuss the different types of energy by having students sort types of energy into seven categories: **light, heat, sound, chemical, mechanical, elastic,**

electrical. Explain that all energy can be divided into two forms: potential energy and kinetic energy.

3. Review the activity by writing the seven types of energy on the board. Bring in objects from home or your classroom and ask kids to sort the objects by energy type. You can also give them a word on a sticky note and have them post the note to the associated type of energy.
4. Create a station in the classroom for each type of energy and give each one a color. Place examples at each station of the type of energy represented there.
5. Divide your class into seven groups. Ask them to explore each station and record their discoveries and questions on the colored paper associated with each station.
6. After the stations activity, post their discoveries from each station. Do a gallery tour and discuss the discoveries and the questions that came out of each exploratory station.

Processing Activities: Going Deeper

Student instructions

1. Research the natural resources in your area and which ones are declining or depleting. What is the story of this decline?
2. Research one way that your community is already finding creative ways to conserve energy and to use what you naturally have around you.
3. Research how the Indigenous peoples of your area have already harnessed the natural resources in sustainable ways.
4. List the innovations in your area. What is the source of energy? Solar powered? Biofuel? Geothermal? Wind? Waste energy? Wave energy? Human powered?
5. What is the story of this innovation? What are possible solutions?
6. Tell the oral story of your research using cue cards or note cards.

Transforming Activity: How Does Energy Transform?

Student instructions

1. Research a template for a pinwheel. Create a pinwheel using only the materials provided by your teacher.
2. Attach the pinwheel to a little car or plastic toy boat. With just the wind blowing, can the pinwheel convert wind into energy that moves the car/boat?
3. Have a race using only wind energy! How will you generate or harness wind energy?

Extensions: Your Turn to Innovate!

The big question is: How can the sources of energy abundant in your area be converted for good use?

1. Choose an energy source that is abundant or readily available in your area.
2. Create an imaginary system that will convert this energy into a sustainable form. Let your imagination soar!
3. Create a pamphlet describing your innovation and how it will help conserve or convert energy.

CORBIS IMAGES

Almost all energy comes from the sun. And solar panels are just one of many ways to harness Earth-friendly energy.

MANWOLSTE/ISTOCK.COM

Book Title: *Every Last Drop: Bringing Clean Water Home* by Michelle Mulder

Big Idea: Water is an essential element of life on Earth. We can trace through different cultures around the world, from the Minoans to the Romans, how water has been used and protected throughout history.

Unit Guiding Questions: How do different cultures preserve their water sources? Which technologies share water? How can water be recycled?

Lesson Goals: I can identify sustainable water-treatment practices here and in other parts of the world. I can describe the distribution of fresh and salt water on the globe and how this affects the lives of others around the world.

Connecting Activities: All the Earth's Water

1. Fill a bucket with water. Explain that this is Earth's water. Then take one tablespoon of water and drink it! Explain that this one tablespoon is the percentage of fresh or drinkable water on Earth. The rest is salt water! What does this mean for all the people on Earth who need water to survive?
2. Read chapter 2 in pairs, small groups or as a class. Have different readers read each part, and have others analyze the photos.
3. Research the drinking-water source in your area. Can you find a reservoir? Where does the sewage go? Draw a map of the water cycle in your area. Where is the water-treatment plant near you?
4. Research the websites *Ryan's Well Foundation* and the *Obakki Foundation*. What did you learn about the people of Africa and their access to clean drinking water?

Discussion Points: Drinkable Water

How clean is the water in your school? Your school district should have facts for public viewing about the water quality in your school. Study the water-quality table as a class. How many flushes are needed before water is considered drinkable? If you are in a new building, it is probably fine! If you are in an old building, what metals are in your school's drinking water, and at what levels?

Processing Activities: Riding the Water Cycle

Student instructions

1. Read chapter 2, "Riding the Water Cycle." Use the "*Every Last Drop:* Water Cycle" handout. Describe what you know through diagrams and words. (*Hint*: Look closely at the diagram in the "Dinosaur Drinks" section on page 19.)
2. Look at the "Water Fact" on page 11. Using the "World Map" handout, create a legend that depicts these facts. Make sure you use a different color for population and for the percentage of fresh water used!
3. Read the section "Swamping the Swamps" in chapter 2 (page 21). What is the purpose of wetlands (swamps or marshes)? Is there a wetland in your area that local citizens are trying to preserve? What other places in the world have natural swamps or wetlands that are used as fresh-water sources?
4. Read the section "All Bottled Up" in chapter three (pages 32–33). What are the dangers of private companies owning drinking water? Is clean water a right? Or a privilege?
5. Look at the "Water Fact" in the "Gulping Weather" section of chapter 4 (page 36). What is your opinion about golf courses?
6. What did the kids in Matamoros, Mexico, do to conserve water? Would any of these strategies work in your school or town? Why or why not?
7. In chapter 3, many different forms of water purification around the world are explored. Using the "Filtering Water Research" handout, list as many different forms of purification as you can and the pros and cons of each. Use logic! There are no right or wrong answers.

Transforming Activities: Research Poster

Teacher instructions

Divide the class into six groups to create six posters that can be displayed in your school hallways. Each poster should support one idea for conserving water in your school. Use the suggestions on pages 40–41 if you need ideas. Use the "Project Proposal Outline" handout.

Student instructions

1. After reading the book, list five things you can do to conserve or protect water.

2. Find examples in your community of initiatives already happening to support this value. Brainstorm one initiative that you could spearhead in your school.
3. Create a pamphlet for your school about how to conserve water. Use the "Brochure" graphic organizer to help!
4. Make water-bottle art! Collect water bottles from the recycling bin in your school. Design and create a water-conservation mascot out of water bottles. What is his/her name? What is his/her message?
5. Canada is home to 70 percent of the world's mining companies. Which mining companies are using responsible mining techniques? Write a letter to a company that needs to be encouraged not to mine in ways that threaten our water supply. Make note of whether you get a response.

Extension: Water Challenge

1. How can you encourage your neighbors to use less water? Do they have a lawn? In what ways can you help them create a sustainable garden?
2. Can you create some nontoxic cleaning products at home? Have you ever used baking soda to clean the bathtub or shower instead of using chemicals?
3. No shampoo! Challenge your classmates or fellow students to not wash their hair for one week (you can rinse with vinegar only!). Research natural ways of cleaning your hair instead of using shampoo. How much water did you conserve in just one week as a whole class?

Stop! Catch that rain! Rain barrels can save families hundreds of liters of water every year.
ZYGIMANTAS CEPAITIS/SHUTTERSTOCK.COM

Book Title: *Pedal It!: How Bicycles are Changing the World* by Michelle Mulder

Big Idea: Bikes are more than transportation. They can be life-changing tools that relieve problems like pollution, make electricity to power machines such as computers and medical equipment, and allow people to earn a living and get an education.

Unit Guiding Questions: How did the invention of the bicycle affect society? How has this invention inspired other inventions around the world? Why are bikes important to communities, nations and countries around the world?

Lesson Goals: I can articulate the history of the invention of the bicycle. I can communicate how the bicycle can relieve several global problems around the world and increase social and economic connections.

Connecting Activity: Bikes!

Show or draw a picture of a bicycle on the board. When and how were bicycles invented? What are the environmental and economic benefits of riding a bike?

Processing Activity: How Do We Commute?

1. Draw a map using different-coloured arrows for each member in your family to demonstrate the distances and type of transportation they use each day of the week.
2. Create a graph that shows how far each member of your family commutes each week and by which means of transportation. Plot the relationship between the total weekly distance and the individual household members. Miles or kilometers are listed on the vertical line, and family members/ transportation modes on the horizontal line. What did you discover? What changes would you like to suggest to your household?

Transforming Activity: Maker Challenge

Bring in recycled goods that are circles or discs. These could be old CDs or coffee-cup tops. Using only tape, cardboard, rubber bands and found or recycled objects, create a two-, three- or four-wheeled vehicle that can move. How do the rubber bands create momentum? How much weight can your vehicle carry before it crumbles? Can it move in water? Take pictures of your inventions and create an engineering challenge for the grade below you.

Extension: We Haul 2 Play

Research the organization We Haul 2 Play (wehaul2play.com). Why do you think that bikes are used to transport sporting goods to communities? Is there a way that bikes could be part of a local initiative to provide needed equipment to your local communities? What can your school do to donate and deliver used equipment to communities in need?

In most countries, bicycles are an important way for adults to get around, but that doesn't stop these Vietnamese girls from trying them too.

STEPHEN BURES/DREAMSTIME.COM

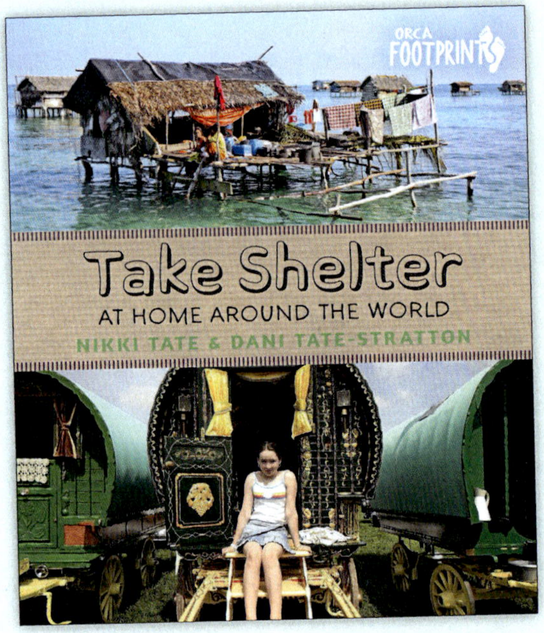

Book Title: *Take Shelter: At Home Around the World* by Nikki Tate and Dani Tate-Stratton

Big Idea: Shelter is a basic human need. Shelters are as diverse as the people who live in them, and they reflect particular climatic and socioeconomic conditions.

Unit Guiding Questions: How does architecture affect the way we live with others? What does housing say about our values and beliefs? What kinds of dwellings and homes support smaller footprints and interdependent communities?

Lesson Goal: I can identify different forms of shelters around the world and how they meet the needs of the people living in them.

Connecting Activity: Scavenger Hunt

Teacher instructions

Write the following questions on the board and ask students to answer them after reading chapter 1, pages 8–9. The answer key is in italics after each blank.

1. According to archeologists, there are two types of cave dwellings: the ____________ *(cliff house)* and the ____________ *(cavete)*.
2. What is the name of the village in Iran where people still dwell in caves? ____________ *(Kandovan)* What are the cave deposits made from? ____________ *(dormant volcano)*
3. What is a kekuli? ____________ *(winter house for Interior Coast Salish in British Columbia)*
4. What do we call a person who lives in a cave or belongs to a cave-dwelling community? ____________ *(troglodyte)*

Connecting Activities: Housing for Us All

Student instructions

1. After reading chapter 3, name five different ways that houses can be built using natural or recycled materials.
    a. If you were to choose one, what would you chose?
    b. Draw a picture of your ideal home that follows these principles of sustainability.

2. Read chapter 4 and then do one or both of the following:
    a. Design your dream home. *Guiding questions:* What materials would you use? How do your choices speak to your values?
    b. Now research high-density housing. Design a building that accommodates many community members in a way that is respectful of privacy and still builds community. What did you discover? Share your blueprints with the urban planners in your city or town.

Transforming Activity: What Inspires You?

Research one of the websites in the "Resources" section (page 44). Write a report about one aspect of architecture, building or design that you find particularly inspiring!

Extensions: Helping Others

1. What do you think about the Ikea flat-pack homes designed for families who have endured a natural disaster and have been forced to live as refugees?
2. Design a flat-pack disaster house for a small family. List the essential items to fill the contents of the flat-pack home.
3. Have you ever volunteered to sort donated goods into shipping containers for responsible charities? Research the Compassionate Resource Warehouse (crwarehouse.ca/ongoing-donation-needs). What can you do to help?

The phrase Home, Sweet Home *reminds us that a house is more than just a place to fall asleep each night.*

PIXELROBOT/DREAMSTIME.COM

Book Title: *Dive In!: Exploring Our Connection with the Ocean* by Ann Eriksson

Big Idea: Our oceans are an integral part of our planet and our survival. There are many ways that we can restore the health of our oceans and preserve marine life through our actions.

Unit Guiding Questions: How are we connected to the ocean? How are oceans a living ecosystem that requires care? What solutions can we imagine to help the health of our oceans?

Lesson Goals: I can define, in my own words, what an ocean ecosystem is. I can articulate how the laws of ecology apply to our oceans with specific examples from around the world.

Connecting Activity: Personal Glossary

Go to the glossary at the back of the book. Pick out ten words that capture your interest or that you are not familiar with. Discuss your words with a friend. As you read the book, create definitions, using your own words, for the terms you have chosen.

Processing Activity: Bingo!

Teacher instructions

As a class, create a bingo game. Have each student create a 3x3 bingo card. Each student will write the ten words from their personal glossary in the boxes. Choose twenty words from the glossary. Have a student read out the twenty terms from the glossary in random order. Can each bingo winner describe the meaning of their terms?

Processing Activity: A Clean Game

Create a board game that draws on the ways we can clean or preserve our oceans. For example, can you create a game like Monopoly in which the winner is the person who accumulates the most points for cleaning our oceans?

Processing Activity: The Four Laws of Ecology

Student instructions

1. What are the four laws of ecology? For each law, what examples can you think of that connect to your own life?
2. Fold a piece of paper in quarters and label each quadrant with one of the laws of ecology. In each quadrant, draw or list ideas that relate to that law.
3. After reading the book, name eight things you can do to help clean our oceans and restore habitats. Post your lists in your school so that others are inspired to respond to this call for action.

Transforming Activities: Plastic Reduction

After reading the book, it is clear that reducing our use of plastics is essential.

1. Create a campaign including posters and flyers that will encourage your local businesses to reduce their use of plastics. Are some businesses already actively reducing their use of plastics? Report back to your class with your neighborhood research.
2. Organize an ecological community cleanup event in an area that needs recovery. It could be a back alley, community park, garden or beach. Can you find sponsorship to support this community event?

Extensions: Get Creative

1. Write a short story from the point of view of a sea creature. What obstacles, struggles and challenges does this creature face? What dilemma or conflict arises that threatens its livelihood? How does the story resolve? What solutions or understandings are provided at the conclusion of your story?
2. Draw pictures to accompany your story, and don't forget to include an afterword to explain the real risks your sea creature faces. Can you list some statistics or facts? Share your story with a younger age group, or donate your book to another classroom so they can learn too!

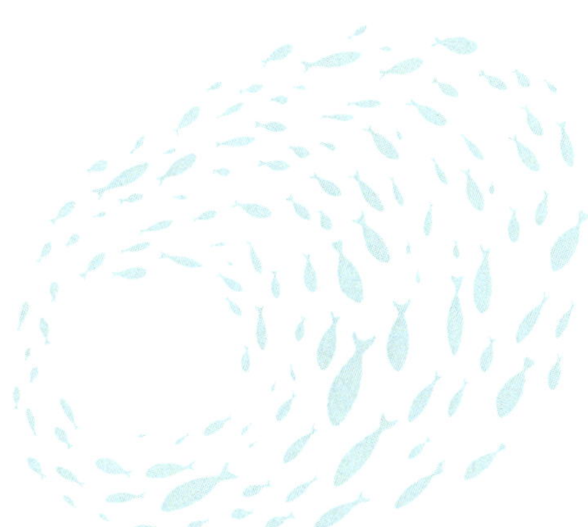

LEARNING CLUSTER THREE: OUR GLOBAL COMMUNITY

This unit invites a close reading of four books that focus on the concept of global citizenship through the sub-themes of sustainable consumerism, fair trade and building global community. The following lessons are suggested activities that are designed to reach all of the learners in your differentiated classroom. The mini unit could be used as a springboard for a larger, long-term unit of study around social justice, innovation, entrepreneurship and social studies.

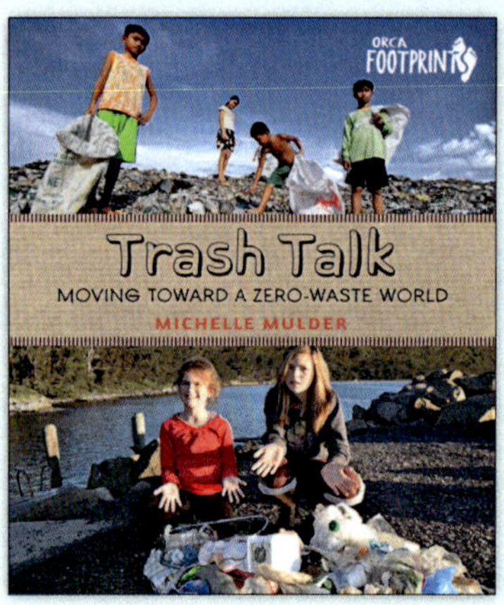

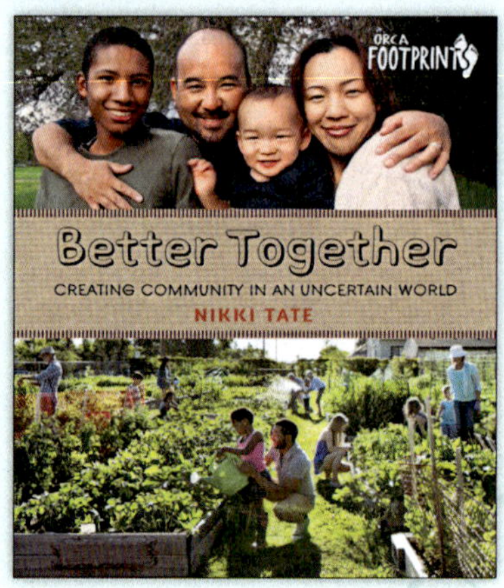

Book Title: *Pocket Change: Pitching In for a Better World* by Michelle Mulder

Big Idea: Sustainable consumerism depends on ethical global economies.

Unit Guiding Question: What does sustainable consumerism look like to you? To your school?

Lesson Goal: I can track and analyze consumer habits in my family.

Discussion Questions:

1. Do you need a bike to freecycle? Why or why not?
2. What is microlending?
3. Is it possible to live without using money? How?
4. Why was money invented?
5. How did the invention of steam engines and factories change how people shopped?
6. How did the arrival of electricity in the 1920s change the way people shopped?

Connecting Activities: Buy It?

1. Ask your family to save a week of receipts. What patterns can you see in the receipts? Where do you buy food? How often? What other household items were purchased? From where? Start a conversation at home about the consumer habits in your immediate household/family.
2. Read chapter 3. What is already growing around you? What are the natural foods/resources that are growing in your area right now? What grows naturally by each season in your area? Interview Indigenous knowledge keepers in your territory. They know!

3. Look at the six actions named in chapter 4 and name one initiative in your school that already takes one of these actions:
   Grow it!
   Borrow it!
   Swap it!
   Sweat it!
   Use kid power!
   Tell 'em what you think!

Processing Activities: To Consume or Not to Consume

Student instructions

1. Draw a timeline of the history of consumerism as outlined on pages 1–17.
2. Media tracking: On a given day, how many advertisements did you encounter? On TV? On social media? On the radio? On signage? In print media? What products were advertised? (See the "*Pocket Change:* Advertisement Tracking" handout.)
3. Examine one photo from chapter 3. What strikes you about the idea behind the picture? What does it make you think about in your own life? Create a collage with the picture that inspires you, and write about how this makes you think about living differently. Give some clear examples of how you might live differently.
4. Create a research poster for your school that describes one of the six actions listed in chapter 4. Be sure to use images, research, graphs and catchy phrases to describe your topic.
5. Create a business plan for one of the six actions described in chapter 4 (for example, "Swap It" on pages 42–43). Is there a local business that has already thought this strategy through? Create an agenda for your first board meeting. What information and discussion topics would be necessary to start this business plan?

Transforming Activities: Where in the World...?

1. Look at the labels on the food in your fridge. Are the strawberries from California? Are the grapes from Mexico? Using the "World Map" handout, draw arrows representing where all the food in your lunch comes from.
2. Research an initiative in your neighborhood, town or city that already uses a community model to trade goods, feed a neighborhood or creatively produce tools for sustainability.

Book Title: *A Fair Deal: Shopping for Social Justice* by Kari Jones

Big Idea: Fair trade is a way of doing business that acknowledges how we are all connected around the globe through trade and commerce.

Unit Guiding Questions: How do my actions affect others around the world? Why does fairness matter? What are some small ways I can positively affect social and economic changes for others?

Lesson Goal: I can identify consumer patterns and demonstrate cause and effect.

Discussion Questions:

1. What is a supply chain?
2. Why are co-ops a good idea?
3. How does fair trade help children?
4. Who started Ten Thousand Villages? Why?

Connecting Activities: Farm to Table

1. Look at the diagram on page 9. How does the farm-to-table movement in the restaurant industry alter this diagram? (Use the **"*A Fair Deal:* Crop-to-Table Graphic Tracker"** handout.)
2. Make a list of all the items available in your school vending machine or school store. On a world map (use the **"World Map"** handout), color-code four items that you can trace. Research which one of these items can be purchased through fair trade. See fairtradecertified.org.

Processing Activities: What's in Your Fridge and Closet?

1. Research one item in your fridge. Draw a crop-to-table diagram of the various stages that item had to go through to get to your table.
2. Research the factory conditions of one corporate retail outlet in your town or city. What statistics did you discover?

Transforming Activities: What's Fair Is Fair

Student instructions

1. Interview a local business owner who has made an effort to consume or use locally made products. Use the **"*A Fair Deal*: Interview Questions"** handout to guide your interview. Can you record the interview and transcribe it later?
2. Research a fair trade store in your town, city or country. What companies are already certified as fair trade?
3. Write a letter to your local Parent Advisory Committee and your administrative team, persuading them to use fair trade products in your cafeteria or vending machine. Provide data, and appeal to their emotions. Create a petition using a list of ingredients or substitutions that come from local products and growers.
4. Cut the tags out of several pieces of clothing that you own. Using the map, glue the tags on the map to show how far your clothes have come to be worn by you! On the legend, calculate the number of miles/kilometers each item traveled to get to your drawer. Consider culling all the clothes you don't wear anymore. Where can you donate them? Are there local establishments that make sure donated clothes are given to people in need?

Extension:
Have each child video their interview about local fair trade business initiatives, and edit the videos as a class.

People all around the world enjoy shopping at markets where they can meet farmers and eat the freshest fruit and vegetables.
MEINZAHN/SHUTTERSTOCK.COM

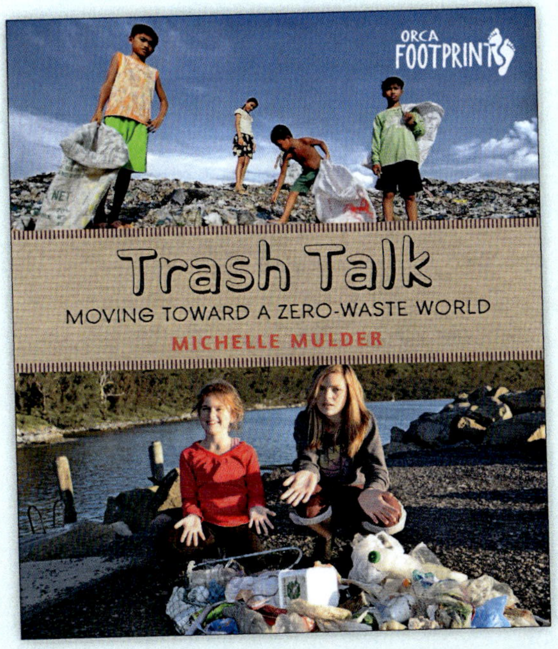

Book Title: *Trash Talk: Moving Toward a Zero-Waste World* by Michelle Mulder

Big Idea: People are natural problem solvers. By sharing more and needing less, we begin to imagine communities based on the values of equity and compassion. This book focuses on how we can deal in a sustainable way with the garbage we produce.

Unit Guiding Questions: What ways can I reduce, reuse and recycle the items in my household? How does one identify a need from a want? What steps can we take to create a zero-waste community?

Lesson Goals: I can identify the top ten types of human garbage and where they end up. I can list the negative impact of landfills. I can imagine one way our school could become a zero-waste community by one year from now.

Connecting Activities: It's Garbage!

Yuck! Let's look through the garbage...

1. Have students look in your classroom garbage can and categorize the items in the trash. Are there paper products? Compost items or biodegradable items? Are there landfill items?
2. Using the "***Trash Talk*: What's in Your Trash?**" handout, categorize the items from the bin in your class, or from another trash bin in your school, into sections. Or divide the class into groups and give them a small garbage can each. Remember to use gloves!

Discussion Point:

What is the most prevalent form of garbage in your school?

Processing Activities: It's All About the Recycling

Teacher instructions

1. Research the dump or landfill closest to your school. Take a trip there as a class or make a call on speakerphone to the manager and ask some questions.
2. Generate ten questions for your local dumping facility around its usage.

3. Research your city or community for information about your recycling program. Take a trip to the facility as a class, or come up with ten questions for a staff member.
4. Research a recycling or upcycling business or community initiative in your neighborhood. Is there a free store near you? What is involved in volunteering for or supporting this project?
5. Read chapter 4 together and complete the comprehension questions individually or as a group (see the "*Trash Talk:* **Comprehension Questions**" handout).

Student instructions

1. After reading the book, choose one project or initiative that caught your eye. It could be from a fact box or a photo with a caption. If you have access to a computer, research this project to get more information.
2. After investigating, use the "*Trash Talk*: **Research**" handout to describe this initiative or project.
3. Present your project to the class or small group.
4. Create a class binder or zero-waste catalog so others can read about the exciting projects happening around the world to decrease our landfill trash!

Transforming Activity: Make Art

1. Take the predominant form of trash in your school and decide how to make it into a group art project.
2. Bring in an old CD and trace a mandala on the shiny part. Color, hang or make a classroom mobile.
3. Bring in an old T-shirt from home. With just a pair of scissors and some imagination, rework, cut, tie and design an updated look.
4. Do you have access to a sewing machine? Can you hand-sew? Take several pieces of clothing and make them into something new. Research upcycled clothing on any "Do It Yourself" website.

Extensions: Recycle!

1. Research which artists in your community have already created art using upcycled or recycled materials.
2. Go through your closet and put aside clothing that is too small or that you haven't worn in a while. Take the unstained and gently used clothes to your nearest shelter, single-parent resource center or donation center. With the stained or ripped clothes, create an installation that signifies a social, political, economic or environmental incident or crisis.

Book Title: *Better Together: Creating Community in an Uncertain World* by Nikki Tate

Big Idea: Building community involves accepting differences in one another and offering our unique strengths to contribute to a healthy, productive world. Diversity and inclusion are features of thriving communities, both economically and socially.

Unit Guiding Questions: How does diversity strengthen community? What does a global community look like and feel like? What growth mind-set do I need to envision more supportive communities?

Lesson Goals: I can define human needs. I am aware of my own personal and social needs and how these needs affect others. I can identify how humans are part of a broader ecosystem. I can give examples of ethical behavior and values from different communities.

Discussion Questions:

1. Why is it hard to concentrate on schoolwork when you haven't eaten breakfast?
2. Why does moving stress our bodies?
3. Why are friendships so important to teenagers?
4. Why do people join community groups?
5. Where does culture fit on your hierarchy?

Connecting Activities: Connectedness

1. Using the **"Circles of Connectedness"** handout, write down the names of people (family, friends, teachers, neighbors, etc.) who fit into your circle. Draw arrows to indicate where you would *like* these people to be in your circle. Use markers to color in areas where there are holes or gaps. Discuss in a small group how you feel about these gaps. See if your friends are able to see connections that you haven't.
2. Using the **"Hierarchy of Needs"** handout, give examples from your life of each area in which you are connected to/provided for.

Processing Activities: Rights for the Children!

1. Research the Charter of the United Nations. In your own words, describe what the charter means. What are some of the values embedded in this charter?
2. Does your country hold some of these values? What examples can you find in policies or federal/state infrastructure that reflect these values? (*Hint*: Look at immigration and health-care services.)
3. Research the "Declaration of the Rights of the Child." What examples can you find from history about children's rights? Find two quotes, reference them, and post them on your classroom wall.
4. Explore the Model UN Activity Guides for kids. Which ones can you recreate in your classroom? (unausa.org/global-classrooms-model-un/for-educators/resources/activity-guides)
5. Exit thoughts: On a sticky note, write one thought/feeling/question you have about children's rights. Pin it on the bulletin board in your classroom.

Transforming Activities: Becoming Change Agents

3. Read chapter 4, "Around the Globe."
4. Describe one initiative that caught your eye. Why does this project interest you? What aspect piques your curiosity?
5. Research a local or global initiative that supports social justice. What inspires you about this particular project? Can you instigate this project in your school community? Do you need to tweak this project or simplify it to make it work in your school? How will you educate your school population on the need for this project? How will you encourage participation? What is the end product/result you hope to see?
6. Create a web page or blog about your project. Ask a local news reporting team to visit your school so you can describe why you feel this project is important. Create awareness by communicating with the parents in your community about the importance of this work.

Extension: Be the Change...

Create a club or social support group in your school that seeks social justice and social change. Ask a teacher to sponsor and supervise your group. What ideas can you generate together about how to change a social mind-set in your school, community or country? Remember, Mahatma Ghandi said, "Be the change that you want to see in the world." We are in this together! Let's work as a team!

Tasha Henry has been traveling, writing and teaching for the past twenty years. She is a published writer and poet and holds a Master of Education in Language, Culture and Teaching from York University. She has taught high-school students and has trained teachers across Canada as well as internationally. She currently lives on unceded Lekwungen territory in Victoria, British Columbia.

FATCAMERA/ISTOCK.COM

Frayer Model: Concept Map

(Fold on the dotted lines)

Name: ________________________________

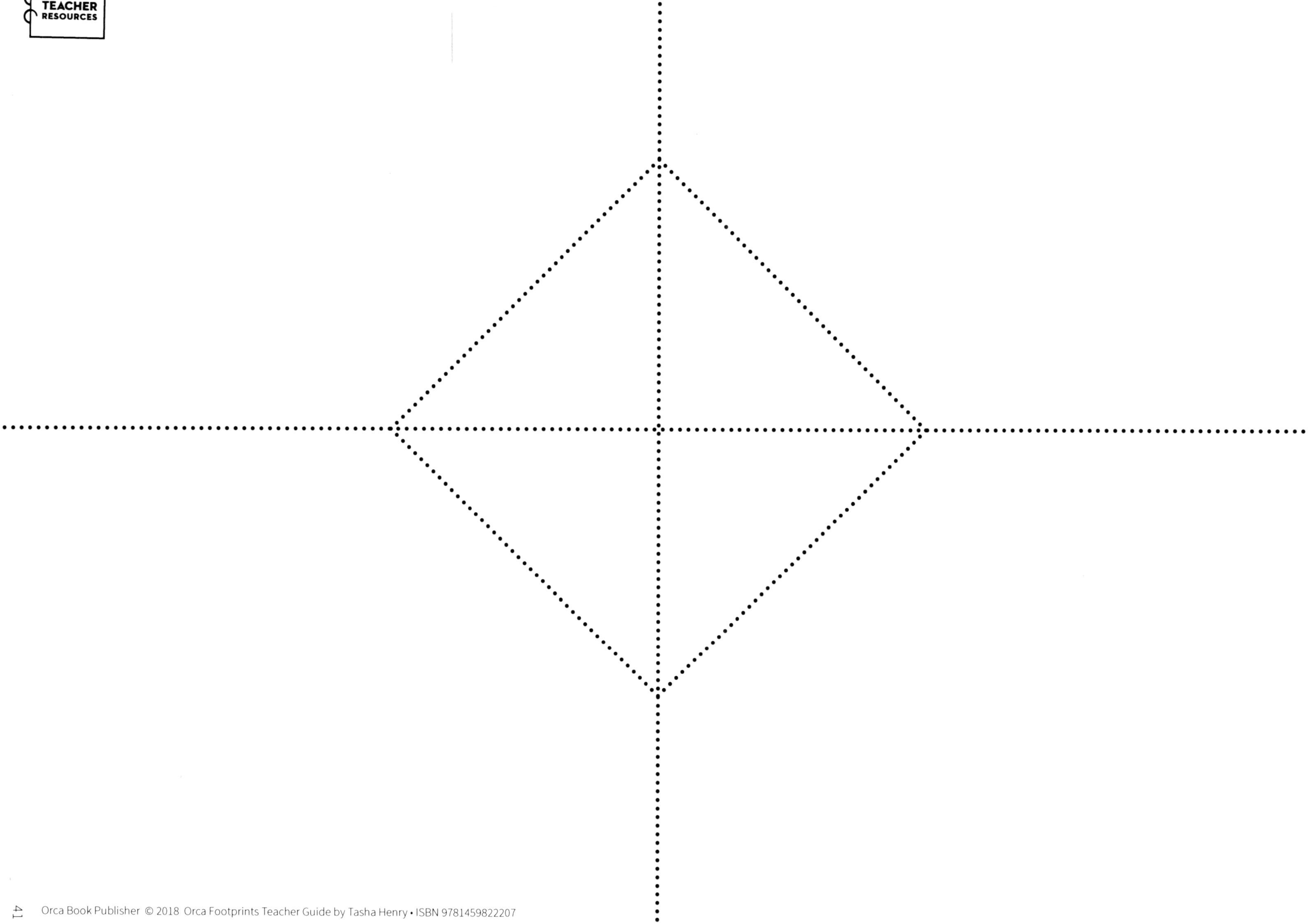

 Orca Footprints Teacher Guide by Tasha Henry • ISBN 9781459822207

Concept Tree

Name: ______________________________

Concept Quadrangle

Name: ______________________________

Definition

Examples in my life

Possibilities

Examples in the world

Orca Book Publisher © 2018 Orca Footprints Teacher Guide by Tasha Henry • ISBN 9781459822207

World Map

Title: ____________________

Name: ____________________

LEGEND

☐	____________	☐	____________	☐	____________
☐	____________	☐	____________	☐	____________

Project Proposal Outline

Main Idea:

Inspiration: ______________________

Message of Project: ______________________

Form of Project:

- ☐ film/video
- ☐ poster
- ☐ brochure
- ☐ essay
- ☐ diorama
- ☐ dramatization
- ☐ slideshow/PowerPoint
- ☐ other

Names:
1. ______________________
2. ______________________
3. ______________________
4. ______________________

Research Grid

Name: ____________________

Interesting Information	Important Facts
Stakeholders	**Is it sustainable? Why or why not?**

Key Question/ Sub-Questions

Name: ______________________________

Key Question

Sub-Question

Sub-Question

Sub-Question

Sub-Question

I'm still wondering...

____

____

ORCA TEACHER RESOURCES

KWL Chart: Thinking Clouds

Name:______________________________

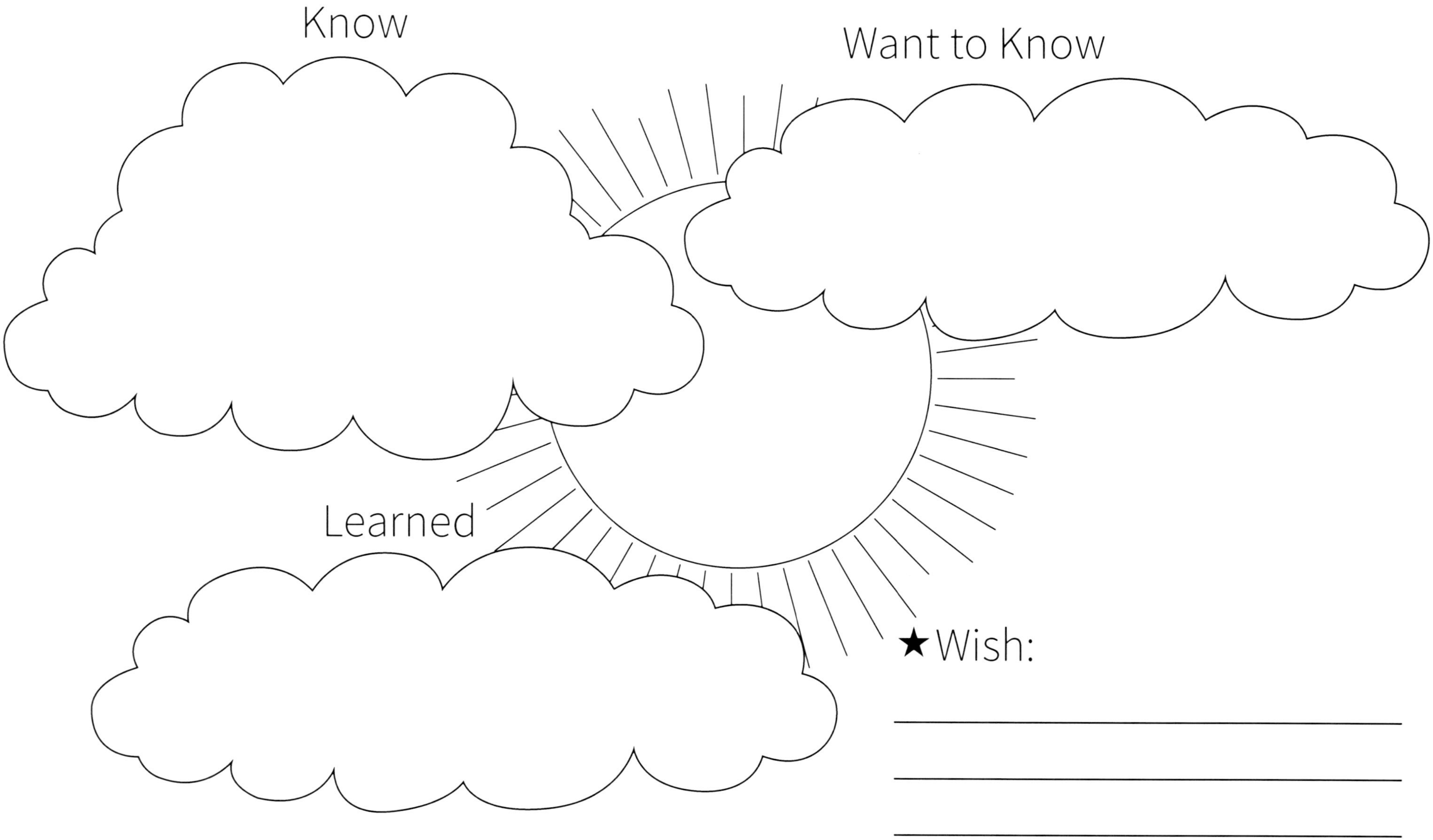

Unit Assessment Demo

Name: ______________________________

I used to think…

I now know…

I can…

I can become…

I secretly wish…

Name: ______________________________

Inquiry-Based Learning Rubric

Highlight the areas in each row that represent your learning:

Project-Based Learning Outcomes	Needs More Work	Approaching Expectations	Meets Expectations	Exceeds Expectations
Knowledge of topic	I understand a few key facts about the topic.	I understand many key facts about the topic.	I understand the complexity of the topic.	My understanding goes beyond the topic and makes connections to other things.
A good question	My question was answered in a yes/no or demonstration.	My question opened up another question that was answered quickly.	My question opened up other questions that couldn't be answered right away.	My question was very complex and brought me to another area of study.
A demonstration that invites public feedback	My demonstration did not address my question.	My demonstration addressed one aspect of my question.	My demonstration addressed all aspects of my question.	My demonstration revealed more than my question.
My reflection	My reflection was just the "bare bones."	My reflection had a few insights.	My reflection showed my analysis and was well crafted.	My reflection was critical and insightful and extremely well crafted.

Comments (can be scribed, typed or drawn)

I used to think ______________________________

____

I now think ______________________________

____

I want to learn more about ______________________________

____

Next time I would ______________________________

____

Self-Assessment Rubric

Highlight the areas in each row that represent your learning:

Name: ______________________

Criteria	Beginning	Practicing	Developed	Applying
Knowledge and understanding (content, ideas, complexity)	I understand the basics of the topic but struggle to offer some evidence or examples.	I understand some of the complexity of the topic. I can give a few pieces of evidence.	I understand the complexity of the topic and can give lots of evidence.	I understand the complexity of the topic and offer some ideas or solutions based on evidence.
Communicating through **form** (sequence, supporting arguments, conclusion)	My work needs a purpose and clarity. I have a beginning, but I need a logical ending.	My work shows a purpose. Some clarity is needed. There is a beginning, middle and end, and it follows some logic.	My work shows a clear purpose. I have a beginning, middle and end, and my conclusion is logical.	My work shows a clear purpose. I have a thesis and supporting evidence and a logical conclusion.
Communicating through **style** (word choice, vocabulary, audience)	My language is clear, simple and the "bare bones." I am working on using more interesting words and descriptions.	My language is somewhat clear, varied and descriptive. I use connecting words and am developing some interesting word choices.	My language is clear, varied and descriptive. I use connecting words and strong vocabulary, and I am aware of my audience.	My language is exceptionally clear, varied and descriptive. I use interesting connecting words and strong vocabulary, and I am aware of my audience.
Communicating through **application** (applying knowledge to a different context or form)	I can demonstrate knowledge in one form and am working on other forms.	I am working on applying my knowledge across contexts using different forms.	I can apply my knowledge across contexts and present it in different forms.	My application of my knowledge is original and impressive.
Understanding through reflection	I am working on analysis and reflection.	I can reflect on my work with some depth.	I can analyze and reflect on the impact of my work.	I can critique my work with depth.

Orca Book Publisher © 2018 Orca Footprints Teacher Guide by Tasha Henry • ISBN 9781459822207

Food-Travel Log

TEACHER RESOURCES

Name: ______________________________

How far does your food travel?

Food Item	From (country)	Distance Traveled (from there to you)
1.		
2.		
3.		
4.		
5.		
6.		
7.		
8.		
9.		
10.		

What is the total number of kilometers/miles traveled for all ten items? ______________

What country/state/province is most of your food from? ______________

What percentage is from your state/province? (*Hint*: Do the math!) ______________

Let's Eat!: Personalized Glossary

Name: ____________________

Concept	In my own words/pictures
permaculture	
organic	
aeroponics	
biomimicry	
ecosystem	
genetic engineering	
aquaponics	
zero-mile meal	
lasagna gardening	

Let's Eat!: Family Menu

Name: ____________________

Directions: Research sustainable food in your area. Create a menu for one week for your household that has the *least* amount of environmental impact. Consider using less meat and less transgenic foods as a start.

Day	AM	PM
Monday		
Tuesday		
Wednesday		
Thursday		
Friday		
Saturday		
Sunday		

Debrief: Discuss with your family the week's meals. What are some pros and cons of sustainable eating?

Food Diary

Name: ____________________

Day	Grain	Meat & Poultry	Dairy	Legumes	Vegetables	Fruit	Fish
1 Date:							
2 Date:							

Notes

 Orca Book Publisher © 2018 Orca Footprints Teacher Guide by Tasha Henry • ISBN 9781459822207

How Kids Feed the World: Word Sort

1

Name: ________________________

Cut out each word on sheet 2 and place it below the right category.

Grain	Meat	Poultry

Other

How Kids Feed the World: Word Sort

2

Name: ______________________________

Cut out each word and place it in the right category on sheet 1.

duckling
wheat
yam
coconut
maize
cassava
pumpkin seeds
rice
ground nuts
soybeans
hen
chicken
ostrich
bovine
ovine
duck
swine
turkey
pigeon

caprine
goat
geese
pig
ox
piglet
dairy cow
sheep
lamb
quinoa
cereal
cashew
hogget
woolly
bulgar
Mangalitsa
popcorn
rhubarb

bee
water buffalo
bison
mozzarella
worm
millet
guinea
emu
flax
quail
moose
peacock
legume
ice cream
chick
rooster
beef
yam

Orca Book Publisher © 2018 Orca Footprints Teacher Guide by Tasha Henry • ISBN 9781459822207

Going Wild: Five-Day Challenge

Name: ____________________

	Personal	Home	School	Neighborhood	Country
Find it!					
Plant it!					
Green it!					
Compost it!					
Rethink it!					

Going Wild challenge description: ____________________

Deep Roots: Our Relationship with Trees

Name: ______________________________

Identify five things for each.

What trees do for us:

1. ______________________
2. ______________________
3. ______________________
4. ______________________
5. ______________________

What we do for trees:

1. ______________________
2. ______________________
3. ______________________
4. ______________________
5. ______________________

 • ISBN 9781459822207

Bees at Work: Fill in the Blanks

Name: ______________________________

1. The male part of the flower is the ______________________, which produces the ______________________.

2. The female part of the flower is called the ______________________ .

When pollen is moved from one plant to another, it is called ______________________ .

3. Trees with needles and cones are called ______________________ .

4. Can animals pollinate plants"? (circle one) Yes No
Describe how this happens.

____

____

____

5. What foods do humans eat that rely on pollination by bees?

____

____

____

6. Out of the 100 or so crops pollinated by bees in North America, only ______________ are pollinated by honey bees.

7. North American farmers use the ______________________ to pollinate almonds, apples, cherries, pears and plums.

8. How do fish depend on bees? ____

____

9. Explain how grizzly bears rely on bees.

____

____

____

Every Last Drop: Water Cycle

Name: ______________________________

Complete the water cycle chart using words/drawings.

___ % is drinkable, fresh water.

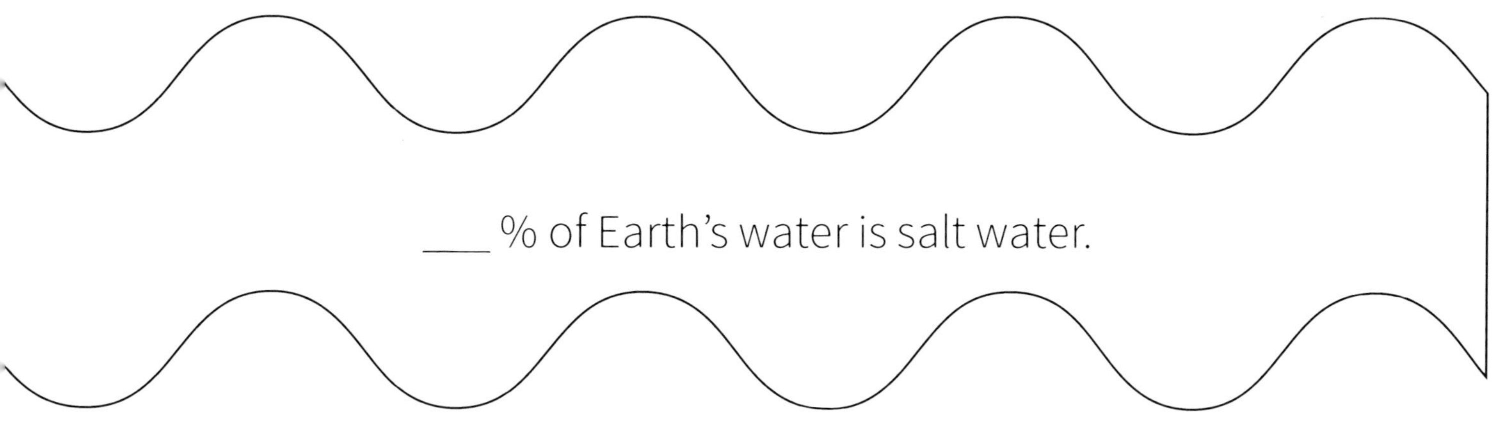

We have had the same amount of water for two years. ___ yes ___ no

Amazing fact: ______________________________

____

ORCA TEACHER RESOURCES

Filtering Water Research

Name: ____

Technique	Pros	Cons
1.		
2.		
3.		

Summary:

My research shows that the most efficient and sustainable form of water filtration in my town/city is

____,

because ____

____

____

____

Actions we can take

Fold second

Resources to investigate

Fold first

Did you know?

1 Brochure

Name: ______________________

Interesting facts

Why it’s important

Pocket Change:
Advertisement Tracking

Name: ____________________

Product	Signage	Social Media	TV	YouTube	Print	Other

Reflection: In my research, I found that ____________________

____

____

____

____

Orca Book Publisher © 2018 Orca Footprints Teacher Guide by Tasha Henry • ISBN 9781459822207

A Fair Deal: Crop-to-Table Graphic Tracker

Name: ______________________________

	Food Item	Food Item	Food Item
	____________	____________	____________
Production	(Location)	(Location)	(Location)
	____________	____________	____________
Distribution	(Location)	(Location)	(Location)
	____________	____________	____________
Consumption			

Reflection:

How many kilometers/miles did each item travel to get to you?

____

____

____

Extension: Using a world map, draw and label each item's journey to you.

ORCA TEACHER RESOURCES

A Fair Deal: Interview Questions

Name: ______________________________

Business owner's name: ______________________________

Business name: ______________________________

Why does your business use local vendors/growers? ______________________________

____

____

____

____

____

What differences is your business making in the lives of others? ______________________________

____

____

____

____

____

Name one product you love. What makes it special? ______________________________

____

____

____

____

____

What are your hopes for consumerism in the future? ______________________________

____

____

____

____

____

Trash Talk: What's in Your Trash?

Name: ______________________________

List and categorize everything in your garbage can.

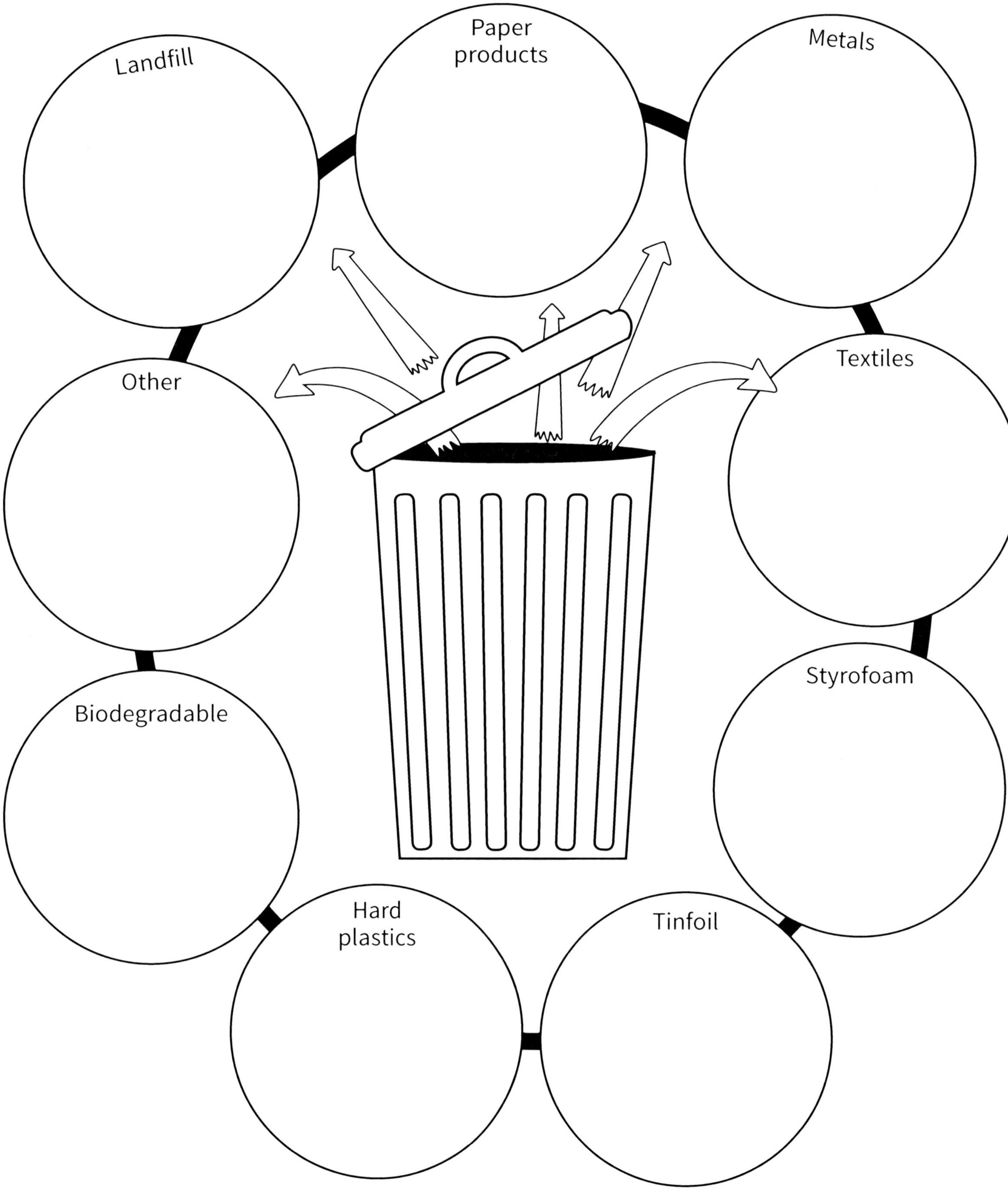

Trash Talk: Comprehension Questions

Name: ______________________________

1. In what year did India ban plastic bags? ______________________________

2. What are neurotoxicants? ______________________________

3. How long does it take for microorganisms to break down vegetable scraps? ______________________________

4. How do repair cafés benefit people of all ages? ______________________________

5. What percentage of communities in New Zealand aim for zero waste? ______________________________

6. Name five ways you can reduce waste in your community.

   a. ______________________________

   b. ______________________________

   c. ______________________________

   d. ______________________________

   e. ______________________________

7. Describe one surprising fact. ______________________________

ORCA TEACHER RESOURCES

Trash Talk: Research

Name: ______________________

Describe one initiative that caught your eye. ______________________

____

____

Where did this project occur? ______________________

____

____

In what year or time frame? ______________________

What/which materials were recycled? ______________________

____

For what purpose or product? ______________________

____

The coolest part of this project to me was ______________________

____

____

One way I could recreate this project in my school/town/city would be to ______________________

____

____

This month I intend to ______________________

____

____

____

____

Circles of Connectedness

Name: ____________________

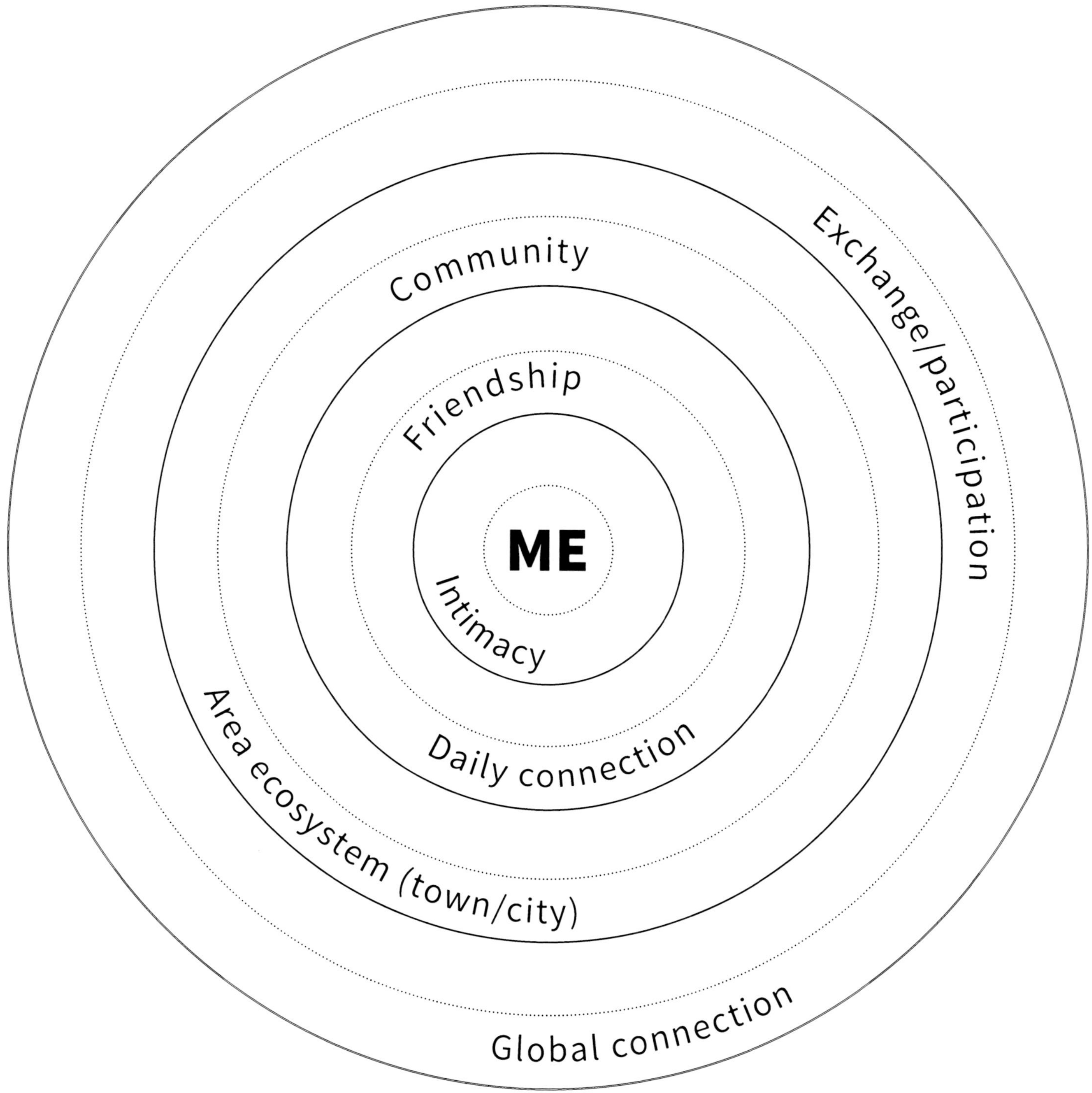

Hierarchy of Needs

Name: ______________________________

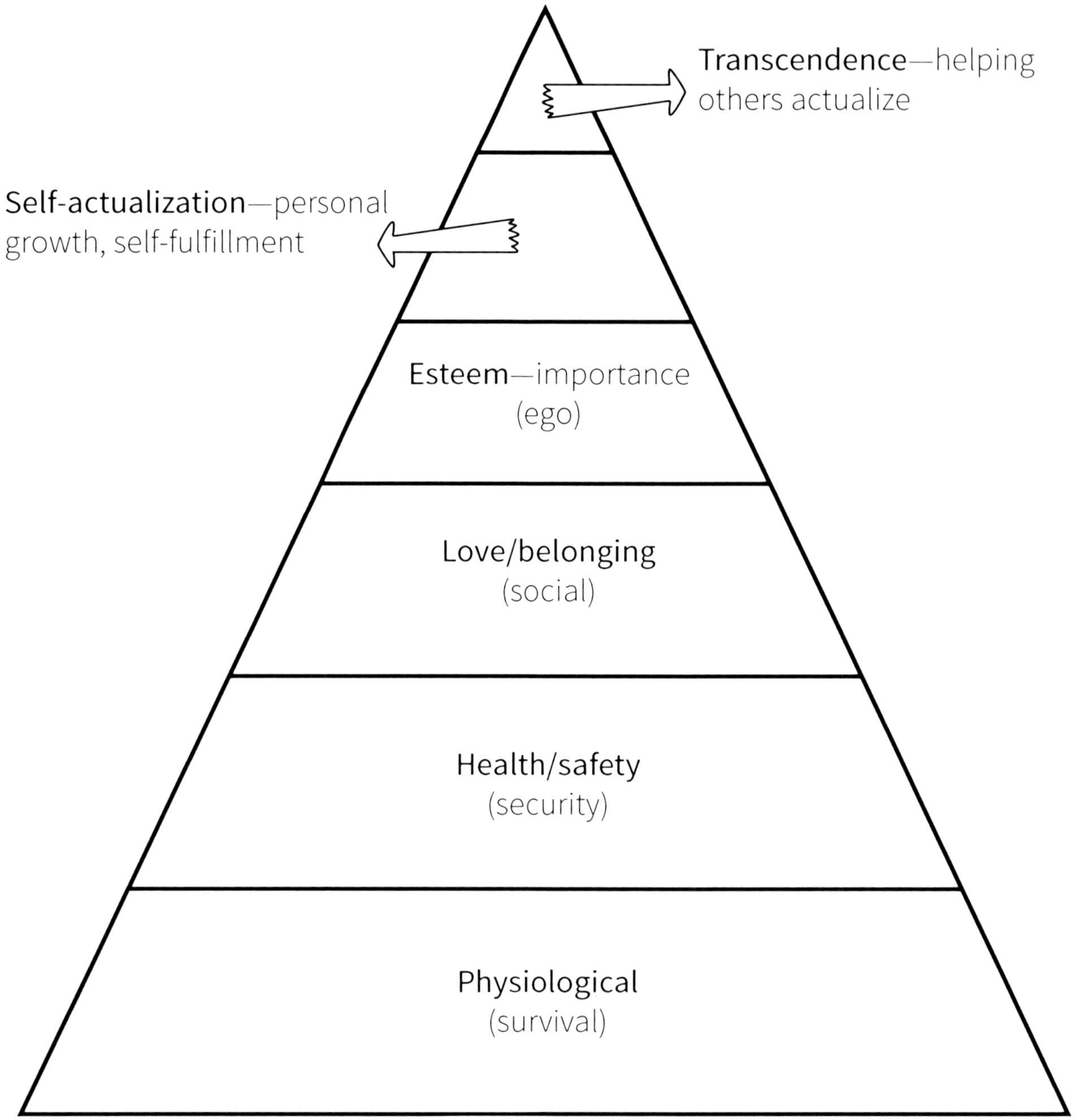

Examples:

Physiological ______________________________

Health/safety ______________________________

Love/belonging ______________________________

Esteem ______________________________

Self-actualization ______________________________

Transcendence ______________________________